How To Win Grins
And Influence Little People

by

Clint Kelly

HONOR
BOOKS

Tulsa, Oklahoma

649.1

How To Win Grins And Influence Little People
ISBN 1-56292-227-0
Copyright © 1996 by Clint Kelly
504 51st Street S.W.
Everett, WA 98203

Cover Image by Penny Gentieu/Tony Stone Images

Published by Honor Books, Inc.
P.O. Box 55388
Tulsa, OK 74155

Introduction

Children, just like grown-ups, need to be reminded how much they are loved and why they are special. If the reminder comes with a creative flair, the impact often lasts a lifetime. These memories can outweigh the fears in life and keep hope in sight.

In this day of cynicism, pessimism, and other "isms," it has become more and more of a challenge to raise children who are filled with self-confidence and have a positive outlook on life. We would all like to become better parents, and we know that part of bringing up children who are confident and determined is to fill them with the knowledge that they are unconditionally loved.

Here are just a few ideas of how to say "I believe in you!" or "You are incredible!" in a whole new way. If you are a parent who has already learned the value of praising your unique child in tangible ways, these may add to your repertoire. If you are just finding out how life-changing and attitude-rearranging a little praise directed toward your child can be, remember: The right thing said at the right time can change your child's life and outlook forever.

And don't just limit yourself to the ideas found in these pages. As you are reading you will begin to think of more specific ways to encourage your "gift from God." Above all, have fun!

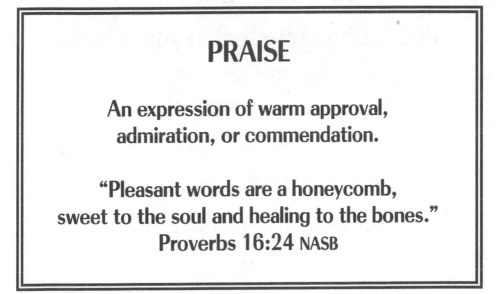

PRAISE

An expression of warm approval,
admiration, or commendation.

"Pleasant words are a honeycomb,
sweet to the soul and healing to the bones."
Proverbs 16:24 NASB

Put washed quarters in your child's birthday cake and let everyone know there's a surprise in it. It sets that cake apart from all others and says, "Here's a little something extra for an extraordinary kid."

✳

Out of the blue, mail your child an invitation to ice cream and bowling, or popcorn and a video. Kids love mail and it shows them you think they are special all the time.

✳

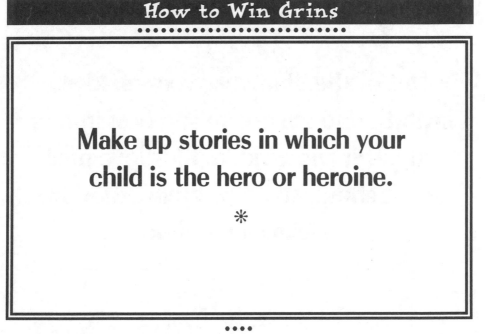

Make up stories in which your
child is the hero or heroine.

✷

Leave a message on the answering machine announcing to all callers that they've reached the home of Mr. and Mrs. John Smith "and their incredibly talented daughter, Linda."

✳

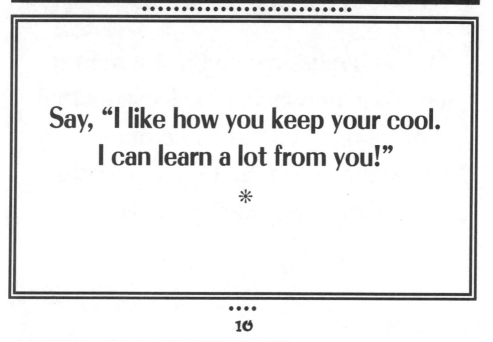

Say, "I like how you keep your cool.
I can learn a lot from you!"

✳

Have a favorite photo of your child blown up to poster size and hang it on the wall in your living room or office.

✳

Present your child with a framed
parchment declaring,
"20 Things I Like Best About You."

✳

Put your arm around your child
and say, "I can't imagine what life
would be like without you."

✳

Declare a "My Special Kid Day,"
throw a party, and invite all your child's
friends. Make it memorable with good food,
exciting games, and a ceremony in which
you tell everyone how important
and accomplished your child is.

✳

Make up or modify a song about your child. If your son's name is Shane, "You Are My Sunshine" easily becomes "You Are My Shane-shine."

✳

When you see your child, greet him
or her with a big smile and say,
"Hi Handsome!" or "Hi Beautiful!"
Give them a hug and add,
"How'd I get such a fabulous kid?"

✳

Take your child to work and show him
or her off to your boss and co-workers.
Treat them to lunch in the company
lunchroom. Over the intercom,
announce the presence
of a "very special guest."

✳

Don't wait for a
Parent/Teacher Conference.
Invite your child's teacher home for
a "Parent/Teacher Celebration."

✳

Believe in your child when he or she is shakiest. Say, "Hey, not to worry. Even Winston Churchill had to repeat sixth grade. Let's see how we can get you over the hump!"

∗

Call the request line at a local radio station and dedicate a song to your child.

*

Tell your child that he or she is "a mighty man of God" or "a mighty woman of God" just like the ones in the Bible. Explain what God can do with someone so special and gifted.

✳

Ask your child's opinion on something major like the purchase of a car or changing jobs. Ask him or her to pray that you'll do the right thing. Then say, "Thanks. Your input is important to me."

✳

Take out an inexpensive ad in the
"Special Occasions" or "Personals"
section of the classifieds:
"Jerry Smith is the World's Most
Special Kid!"

✳

For your child's next birthday party, play the "Cupcake Game." Bake enough cupcakes to spell out how much he or she means to you like "Nate the Great" or "Beth's the Best" with one letter of the message on each cupcake. Scramble the letters and watch the fun as they sort out the sentence.

✳

Tell your child, "You're a much better artist (or speller, or lawn mower, or whatever the truth may be) than I ever was!"

❋

Take your child out for a hot fudge
sundae, or any treat you both love.
Then say, "You know what?
I love you more than a *million*
hot fudge sundaes!"

✳

Put on some favorite music and say, "I would be honored to have this next dance with you!" Let your child stand on your feet. Lots of dips and whirls lead to lots of fun and giggles.

✳

Get them in a "kid sandwich"
and squeeze until "all the ketchup
and mayo run out!"

✳

At bedtime, pretend you're "mailing" them to Grandma—fold, stuff, seal, and stamp them into bed for special delivery. Say, "You know how much Grandma likes to get important mail!"

✳

Let your child ride on your back,
then announce in your best ringmaster
voice, "And now, la-dees and gentlemen,
the moment you've all been waiting for!
The exciting, the talented, the dazzling
Jenny Smith!" Then clap, yell,
and whistle like the roar of a crowd.

✳

Encourage your child to try out
for the school play, then go
to every single performance.

✳

When you come home tired
after work, take your child on
your lap and say, "You know,
you are a bright spot in my day!"

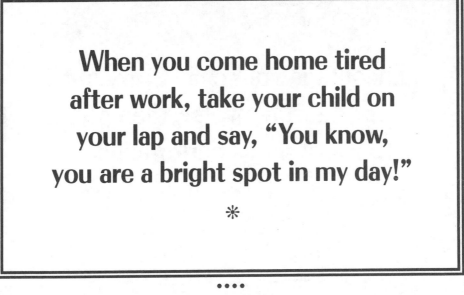

*

Out of the clear blue, say, "I'm so fortunate to be your dad (or mom)!"

*

Keep a special treat drawer
and whenever your child does
something especially well, take him
or her on a visit to the drawer.

✳

Have a T-shirt made with your child's
picture on it and wear it often.

✳

Play Hangman, and use phrases
for your child to guess like:
"Billy is one swell kid!"

✳

Ask for your child's forgiveness.

*

Tell your child what a good friend he or she is. "I can always count on you!"

*

Occasionally do the unexpected.
Let your child stay up past bedtime.
Put cupcakes *and* a candy bar in
their lunch. Speak only in their
secret made-up language.

✳

Take a day off work and "spring"
your child from school.
Go fishing. Go skating. Go!

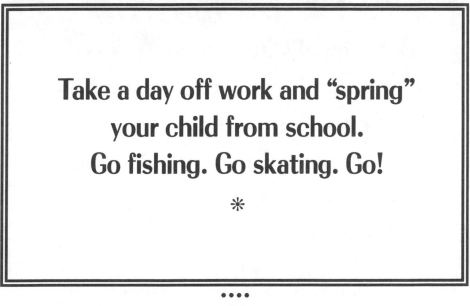

Carry your child's picture
on your key chain.

Teach your child to look up at the clouds. Point at them and say, "One day Jesus will come right through there looking for *you!*"

＊

Say, "No matter what happens, I'm in your corner!"

Take your child into your confidence.
Say, "Thank you for listening.
It means a lot to me."

✳

Make a pitcher of fresh-squeezed
lemonade and put it in the refrigerator
with your child's name on it.

✳

Write up a resume of all your child's accomplishments—big and small. Look it over thoughtfully and say, "I'd hire you in a second!"

✳

Ask your child to laugh for you,
then say, "I love that sound.
It makes me want to laugh too."

*

Grab your child in a bear hug and say,
"You are a living miracle!"

✳

Give 'em a wink and say,
"You are God's reward to me
for eating all my peas!"

✳

Place your hand on your child's head
and pray for him or her aloud by name.
Say, "Thank you, God,
for such a wonderful gift."
Then kiss your gift on the head.

＊

Put a note of praise in a bottle and
float it in your child's bath water.

✳

Say, "Will you come and snuggle with me? I always feel so comforted when you're near."

＊

Keep a supply of popsicles on hand.
When your child does something well,
give 'em a "praise pop."

✳

Cuddle with your kid.
Fall asleep together on the couch.
Let your child feel your physical
support, affection, and protection.

*

Smooch 'em.

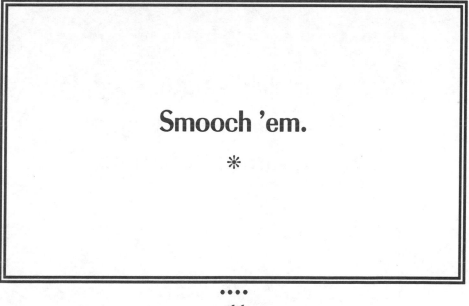

After your child's bath, snuggle him or her and say, "Ummm. You smell fresh from God!"

✳

Have a candlelight dinner for your child. Say, "This is a rare event only reserved for a special guest!"

✳

Help your child to anticipate "Heavenly Praise Day," when he or she shall hear God the Father say, "Well done, good and faithful servant!"

*

Say, "Remarkable! I really admire
you for that!" when your child
does or says something well.

*

Bake "praise cookies" using a fortune cookie recipe. Each time he or she breaks one open, your child will receive a pat on the back like: "You always do such a nice job on the lawn!" or "I like the way you draw!"

✳

Say to your child, "If your smiles were gold, we'd be billionaires!"

＊

Mark your child's growth on the wall with fluorescent smile stickers. Set a reasonable height "target" and tell your child that when he or she hits it, you'll throw a "Growing Up" party.

✳

Include your child's name on all return address labels, personalized stationery, and customized Christmas cards. This says, "You are an important person!"

∗

Send your child a thank-you card
for a job well done. Include a gift
certificate to his or her favorite
fast food restaurant.

✳

Say, "If everyone was as thoughtful as you, the world would be a much nicer place."

✳

Toast your child with ice cold cans of soda. "Here's to Jimmy, a remarkably creative guy. He makes me happy, he makes me laugh, and he makes me glad I'm his mom (or dad)!"

*

"Kidnap" your child from bed on
a Saturday morning and treat him
or her to breakfast at a restaurant.

*

Snuggle in bed together and
listen to an old-time radio
mystery/comedy in the dark.

✳

Climb a tree with your child, then shout to the world, "I have the most spectacular kid on the planet!"

✳

Play the memory game "Mother's (or Father's) Shopping Bag." Make each item that goes in the bag one of your child's talents or good qualities. The person able to repeat the most items in sequential order wins.

✳

Instead of telling your child he or she is a real character, say, "You're a Kid With Character!" Watch your child rise to the compliment!

✳

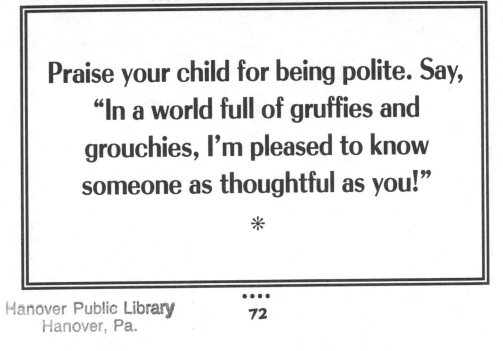

Praise your child for being polite. Say, "In a world full of gruffies and grouchies, I'm pleased to know someone as thoughtful as you!"

✳

Offer to be your child's pen pal
and let him or her write you at work.
Use notes, funny postcards,
and letters as an opportunity
to put your pride in writing.

*

Create a "Star Attraction"
poster board for the kitchen wall
that features your child in the leading
role. Include his or her essays,
art work, and action photos.

❋

For a special treat, declare your child
"Pizza Perfect" and take him or her out
for a triple pepperoni gutbuster.

✳

Use music, art, or sports lessons
as a reward for a job well done or
for a good attitude. That links
learning and encouragement.

*

When your child makes a wise
decision, like choosing carrot sticks
over candy, praise him or her with,
"What a smart choice!
That's using your brain!"

✳

Use your work space as a gallery
for your child's best work.
It links achievement and industry.
Be sure to host a special
"showing" now and then.

*

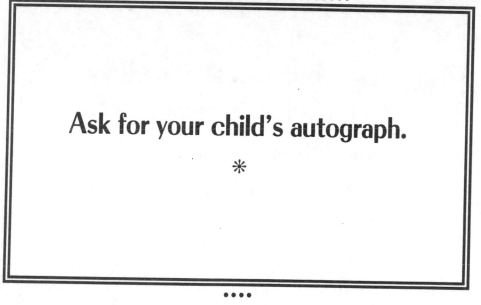

Ask for your child's autograph.

✳

Share your ancestral heritage,
coat of arms, or family motto
and tell your child what an
important family link he or she is.

✳

Let your child choose paint for his or her room in any color combination he or she wishes.

✳

Tell your child, "I have so much faith in you!"

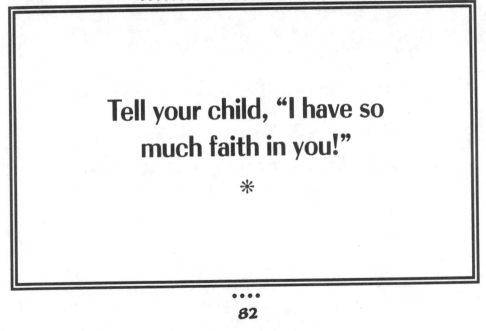

Catch your child's eye across
a crowded room or on the playing
field and give him or her a wink
and the thumbs up sign.

*

Say, "How grown-up you are! You just solved a problem twice your size!"

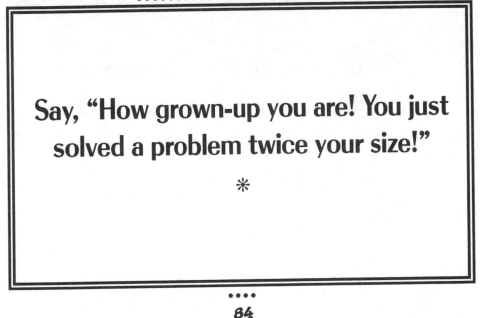

Let your child choose dinner tonight,
shop for the ingredients together,
prepare it together, then declare to
all diners, "This meal is officially
declared Jimmy's Delight!"

✳

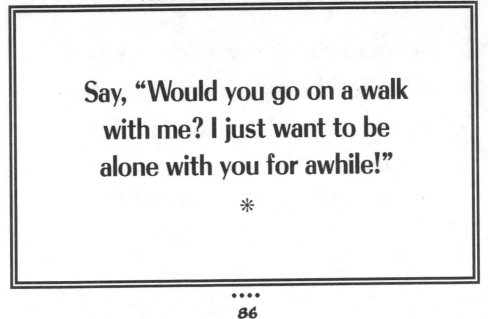

Say, "Would you go on a walk with me? I just want to be alone with you for awhile!"

✳

Compare your child to a favorite
animal: "You're strong as a lion!"
or "You're pretty as a peacock!"

*

Make bookmarks with your child's
school photo. Laminate them,
and give them to family and friends.

✳

Pray aloud with your child
and give God praise for "Billy's"
or "Sarah's" best qualities.

＊

Say, "You acted so kind
toward that person.
Do you feel as good as she does?"

＊

File your child's artwork and essays
in a loose-leaf binder so he or she
can take pride in developing skills.

✳

Say, "You did that so well.
You are going to be a very successful
grown-up. I can see it now!"

✳

Declare two days a month "Praise Daze" in your home. Be spontaneous and allow your child to do something out of the ordinary, like wear mismatched clothes or take a can of whipped topping into the bathtub. It links fun with commendable behavior.

✳

Praise an honest child with, "It took a lot of courage to tell me the truth when you knew I'd be mad."

*

Trace your child on a large piece of butcher paper. Tack it to the wall and have family and friends write words of encouragement to your special one.

✳

Say, "You have the most interesting ideas. What do you think about _____?"

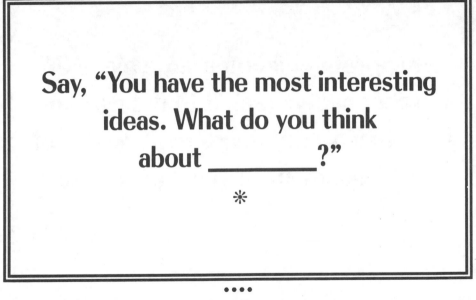

Give your child a Valentine
in August. When he or she gives
you a funny look, say, "You're
special to me *all* year round!"

✳

Attach an envelope to the outside of your child's bedroom door. Mark it "Praise-O-Grams" and periodically "mail" them a note of encouragement.

✳

Say, "I admire the way you did that without complaining."

✳

Blow up a photo of your child on the copy machine and glue it to the front of a box of Wheaties™ cereal, the "Breakfast of Champions."

✳

Tell your inquisitive child,
"You know, you ask the *best* questions.
I'm so glad you're curious
and aren't afraid to ask!"

✳

Catch your child doing praiseworthy things. Write each good thing down on a piece of paper and put it in one space of an empty egg carton. When you have 12 good things, present him or her with One Dozen Grade A Fresh Praises.

✳

Say, "It wouldn't surprise me if
you climbed Mt. Everest or discovered
the cure for cancer. You and God
can accomplish anything!"

✳

Praise achievements. "You worked so hard on that. It's really going to pay off for you someday."

✳

Say, "You're so much fun to be with.
Let's play!"

Create a yummy dessert dish in
honor of your child and serve it
only on special occasions.
Call it "Sam's Favorite Pudding"
or "Carla's Creamy Delight."

✳

Look your child in the eye and say,
"I have great confidence
in your judgment!"

*

Record your child's laughter and play it back once in awhile. Say, "Now *that's* music to my ears!"

*

Let your child chair a family meeting.

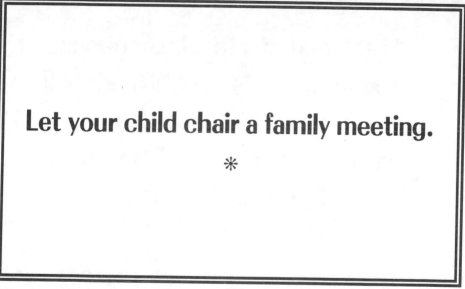

*

At the end of a meal, announce, "And now, for dessert, Wendy will read her favorite poem (or joke, or short story, or...)." Be sure to serve *real* dessert too!

✳

Share a special place with your child
where only the two of you go.

*

Plant a garden of praise together with Terrific Tomatoes, Proud Peas, Courageous Carrots, and Beautiful Beets—and enjoy the harvest!

✳

Use terms of endearment,
no matter how silly they might seem.
"Hey, Sweetcakes, I'm so glad
you're my big girl!" or "There goes
my cool cowboy now!"

✳

Praise the small things. "You tied your shoes very well!" or "You were such a gentleman at dinner tonight, it was a pleasure to sit next to you!"

✳

Leave a note on the bathroom mirror. "Good morning, Brenda, what a fine smile you have!"

*

Rock your child and sing. Give him or her a squeeze and say, "Thank you, Lord, for such a fine package as this!"

✳

Give your child a kiss and say, "Thank you for forgiving all my mistakes!"

✳

Have license plate frames made that say, "I'm the proud parent of Jeffrey Smith!"

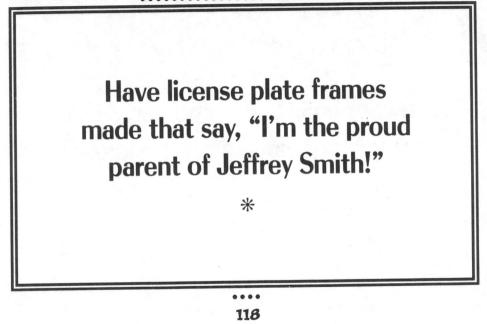

*

Send your child into the grocery store with the money to buy dinner. "Surprise me. Whatever you choose, I'm sure it will be delicious!"

*

Make a videotape of your child's achievements and send copies to selected relatives and friends. Title it "In Celebration of a Special Kid."

*

Encourage your child with "put-ups"
(opposite of "put-downs") like:
"You have one of the most interesting
rooms in the house!" Then comment
on the things that make his
or her room unique.

✳

Sit with your child and look
at a magazine full of pictures and
colorful advertisements. Encourage
your child to point out the things
he or she likes and to tell you why.

✳

Play "Patchwork Story" with your child as the hero. You start the story with a sentence or two, then stop and let your child pick up where you left off—and so on.

＊

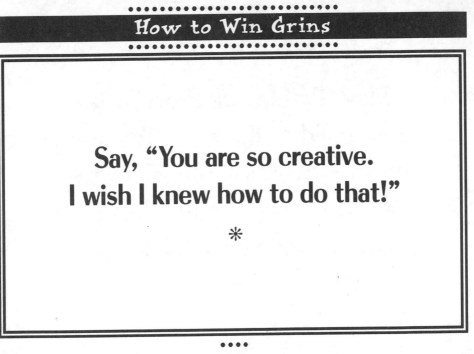

Say, "You are so creative.
I wish I knew how to do that!"

✳

Form a "kitchen band" by letting your child select the "instruments" from food and utensil cupboards and drawers. Perform a "concert" together.

✳

Sit outside under a blanket at night, hug, and marvel at the heavens together. Say to your child, "Wonderful as it is, it wouldn't be complete without you!"

*

Every time your child tells someone about Jesus, say, "My, what beautiful feet you have!" (*How beautiful are the feet of them who bring good news!* Isaiah 52:7.)

✳

Whenever your child does something nice for someone, tell him or her it was a godly thing to do for "God is love." (1 John 4:16)

✳

Play "Character Counts Catch"
with your kid. That's counting
how many times in a week you
catch him or her showing *character*
(i.e., integrity, moral excellence).
"Pitch" them some praise.

✳

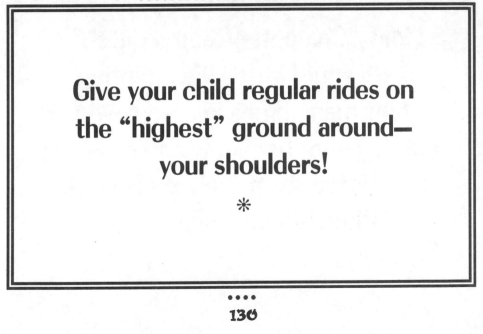

Give your child regular rides on
the "highest" ground around—
your shoulders!

✳

Take 12 photos of your child doing praiseworthy things and have them made into a calendar for his or her wall—and one for yours!

*

Read to your child from books on Abraham Lincoln, Florence Nightingale, and other praiseworthy people. When you come to a quality of the famous person that you've also seen in your child, stop and tell him or her how much that action reminded you of something Abe or Flo would have done!

✳

Save some July 4th sparklers
and set them off with your child
on New Year's Eve. Say, "I can't
think of a better way to start the
year than with you by my side!"

✳

Take your child for a ride in a hot air balloon. Say, "This is to celebrate the fact you make my spirits soar!"

∗

Hunt four-leaf clovers together. Press any you find into a scrapbook titled with your child in mind, like "Timmy's Unique" or "Tammy's Special."

✳

Get silly together by acting out
Dr. Seuss, reciting tongue-twisters,
or having a staring contest.

*

Do something "posh" together, like go to a play, have dessert in a fancy restaurant, or test drive a Cadillac.

✻

Help your child solve a difficult
problem—don't solve it *for* him or her.

✳

Tell each other your "most embarrassing moments" and mark each one with a chocolate kiss.

✳

Slip a "Hug-o-Gram" under your child's bedroom door before he or she wakes up in the morning.

✳

Whenever the "tooth fairy" pays a visit to your child's pillow, make sure she also leaves a note of encouragement: "You have the nicest smile on my route!"

＊

Say, "What do you want to be when you grow up *and how can I help you get there*? You can do it, I just know you can."

✳

Quote Goethe to your child: "Whatever you can do, or dream you can, begin it. Boldness has genius, power, and magic in it."

＊

Take your child by the hand—
and squeeze.

✳

Talk to your young child about news events so that he or she feels an important part of the currents of life—and perhaps less fearful.

✳

Sponsor an orphan in your child's name. Say, "Because you're such a big help to me, I'd like you to meet someone who could sure use your encouragement."

✳

Send a bouquet of flowers to your
child at school, "Just because."

✳

Write a letter to the editor of
your local newspaper and say what
makes yours such a terrific kid.

*

Curl up with your child and let
him or her read to you.

＊

Take your child berry picking and let him or her fill one basket to eat without having to share.

✳

Throw a "praise party" for your child and "invite" all his or her stuffed animals.

✳

Spell out "Super Job" and your child's name in sticks of gum taped to his or her bedroom door.

*

Once or twice a day, set your alarm clock, wrist watch, or oven timer and when the bell or beeper goes off, stop whatever you're doing, find your child, and give him or her a praise hug. Pretty soon, your child will listen for the signal and come looking for you!

✳

Get excited over your child's dreams. When he or she expresses a desire to become a teacher or a chef, take it seriously and brainstorm together for ways to reach the goal.

✳

Record your child's funny sayings
and wise words in a special book.
Read selections at special gatherings
or use them to liven up your
answering machine messages.

❋

Practice optimism. A sunny disposition lets your child know you enjoy his or her company. Watch their self-confidence grow!

✳

Each time your child does something kind, pat your tummy, smack your lips, and say, "My, that was nourishing. Thanks for the vitamin K (for kind)!"

＊

About the Author

Clint Kelly, an adventure novelist and publications specialist for Seattle Pacific University, is a happily married father of four. His articles for kids have appeared in *Breakaway*, *Cobblestone*, and *Child Life* magazines. Kelly's book, *Me Parent, You Kid! Taming the Family Zoo,* is all about effective parenting.

Additional copies of this book and other titles from
Honor Books are available at your local bookstore.

Me Parent, You Kid! Taming the Family Zoo by Clint Kelly
God's Little Instruction Book for Dads by Honor Books
God's Little Instruction Book for Moms by Honor Books
God's Little Devotional Book for Moms by Honor Books
God's Little Instruction Book for Kids by Honor Books
The Children's Topical Bible by Mary Hollingsworth

Other books available from Clint Kelly
are at your local bookstore.

The Aryan
The Landing Place
The Lost Kingdom

Tulsa, Oklahoma